Edna,

CATS CATS CATS

Now you will have time to
play with cats all day.
Enjoy yourself and your retirement.
Love
George
6/98

CATS CATS CATS

a collection of great cat cartoons

EDITED BY S. GROSS

BARNES
&NOBLE
BOOKS
NEW YORK

Some of the cartoons in this collection have appeared in the fol-
lowing periodicals and are reprinted by permission of the authors:
*Audubon, Better Homes and Gardens, Boys' Life, Campus Life,
Cavalier, Cosmopolitan, Diversion, Family Circle, Good House-
keeping, Gourmet, House & Garden, Ladies' Home Journal, National
Enquirer, National Lampoon, 1000 Jokes, Oui, Parade, Penthouse,
Philadelphia Inquirer Magazine, Playboy, Punch, Saturday Evening
Post, Saturday Review, This Week, TV Guide, Vision, Woman's Day,
The Yacht.*

Grateful acknowledgment is made for permission to reprint:

Cartoons by Roz Chast from *Parallel Universes*. Copyright ©
1984 by Roz Chast. Reproduced by permission of the author.
Cartoon by Henry Martin on page 98 from *Punch*. Copyright ©
1983 by Punch. Reprinted by permission of Rothco Cartoons Inc.
and the author.
Cartoons by John S. P. Walker. Reprinted from *Bad Dogs* by John
S. P. Walker. Copyright © 1982 by John S. P. Walker. Reprinted by
permission of Alfred A. Knopf, Inc. and Methuen and Company,
Ltd.
Cartoon by Gahan Wilson on page 78 from *Playboy*. Copyright
© 1972 by Playboy. Reproduced by special permission of *Playboy*
magazine.
Cartoons copyrighted by *The New Yorker* are indicated through-
out the book.

"I guess she's the theme again this evening."

ED FRASCINO

1

"There's a silly sign if
I ever saw one."

"Brace yourself, Grace. The doctor has discovered
the nature of my allergy."

WILLIAM HOEST

SIDNEY HARRIS

"Her landlord kicked her cat!
How did this thing ever get out of Small Claims Court?"

EVERETT OPIE

© 1967 The New Yorker Magazine, Inc.

"Now, don't start complaining till you taste it."

FRANK MODELL
© 1983 The New Yorker Magazine, Inc.

REX MAY (BALOO)

Face gets wild.

Back hunches up.
("Halloween kitty")

Noisy runs after
invisible things.

GALUMPH
GALUMPH

Back to normal.

ROZ CHAST

9

"Could you show me something just a little more scratch-resistant?"

O'NEILL CATHARINE O'NEILL

"Hmm . . . looks like the bottom's falling out of the cat book market!"

11

"Does that include cats?"

"Now we've only two more kittens to unload."

"She has your eyes."

BERNARD SCHOENBAUM

"We have an important visitor today: the King of the Cats."

ED FISHER

SIRACUSA

CATHERINE SIRACUSA

"I hope you don't mind cat hairs."

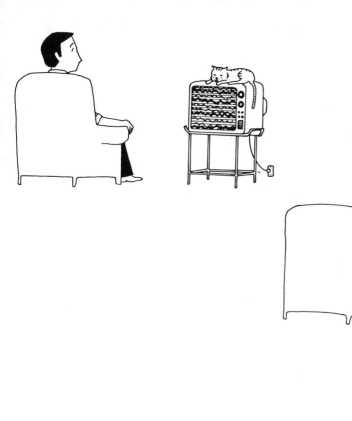

FELIPE GALINDO (FEGGO)

19

THE AMAZING ADVENTURES OF BOB THE CAT AFTER HE WAS PUT TO SLEEP

MICK STEVENS

"I think we'll take it, subject to his approval."

ED FRASCINO

21

CHARLES ADDAMS

"Have you been made to feel welcome?"

MORT GERBERG

"Don't forget to give Gertrude her pill."

24   DON OREHEK

Q: WHAT KIND of CATS ARE MOST FRIENDLY?

A: THOSE WHO HAVE THE WORST BREATH.

OLIVER CHRISTIANSON (REVILO)

25

BERNARD SCHOENBAUM

"Peasant!"

HENRY MARTIN

"Our only consolation is that in about eleven years the controlling stockholder will be dead."

27

1.

2.

3.

P.C. VEY

"You're purring. I like that in a cat."

29

JOHN CALLAHAN

S.GROSS

SAM GROSS

VAHAN SHIRVANIAN

"This is a solo number, if you don't mind."

LEE LORENZ

"We've been living together for six years, toots. How about getting hitched?"

"Did you get a description of the cat?"

ORLANDO BUSINO

THE VIGIL

1

2

3

4

5

6

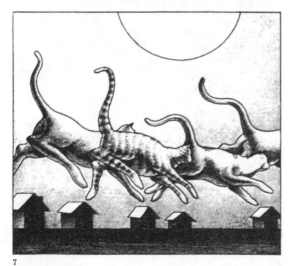

7

8

(continued)

9

10

11

12

36

ED FRASCINO

"I like dogs better. Dogs kiss."

37

P.C. VEY

"Have you ever read the label on a can of cat food? It reads 'all beef and beef byproducts.' . . .
Now tell me, do we look like either beef or beef byproducts?"

"You might as well introduce him to the 'treats' you got last year."

"I *do* apologize, Rinehart. The cat has never bitten anyone previously."

41

"The Graysons are on vacation in Europe. I'm the sitter."

"It's 20 cents a pound cheaper. *That's* why!"

ARNIE LEVIN

"The artist was one of the first to experiment with the use of velvet
as an alternative to canvas."

BILL WOODMAN

45

CAT
BRAIN TEASER

1. Who is your owner?

A.    B.    C.    D.

2. Which of the following is inedible?

A.   B.    C.   D.

3. Name the scratchpost.

A.

B.

C.

D.

4. What happened to your little mouse-toy?

A.

Under couch

B.

Behind bookcase

C.

Turned into a ghost

D.

I don't know and
what's the difference?

R. Chast
ROZ CHAST

47

"Actually it's turned out to be more of a cat feeder."

WILLIAM HOEST

". . . and that's why a cat on a boat
is considered bad luck."

BILL MAUL

48

"He's a confirmed bachelor."

ED FRASCINO

49

"No more Kitty-bits, Jenny.
We're all Seventh Day
Adventists now."

O'NEILL

CATHARINE O'NEILL

50

"What's there to discuss?"

MICHAEL MASLIN

"Who do you think you're staring at!"

"Honey, I think the cat wants out!"

WALTER GALLUP

"He's never been sick a day in his life except for an occasional fur ball."

"Now you tell me you get airsick!"

S.GROSS
SAM GROSS

FELIPE GALINDO (FEGGO)

"He's merely putting the cat out, but he makes such a drama out of doing it."

Noel Watson

ALEX NOEL WATSON

58

LITTLE KNOWN FACTS: A CAT WEIGHS TWICE AS MUCH WHEN IT IS SLEEPING!

OLIVER CHRISTIANSON (REVILO)

TIM HAGGERTY

"Did you know you could throw out your back doing that?"

Anthony

ANTHONY TABER

JO LINKERT

"Good news, Mr. Smith! The cat
got down safely."

61

"Meow! Pass it on!"

62

"He sure fooled me . . . I didn't think he gave a damn about anything."

THOMAS CHENEY

63

ED FRASCINO

"When you told me you were an ailurophile I thought you were into some kind of kinky sex."

"Jonathan!"

DON OREHEK

65

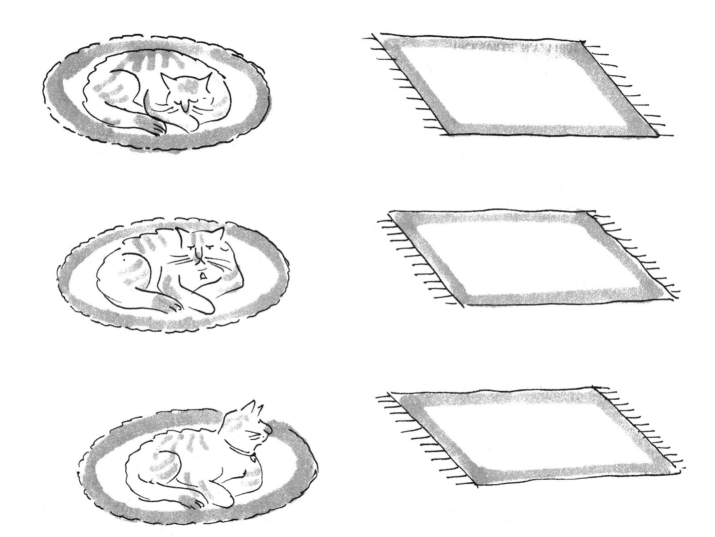

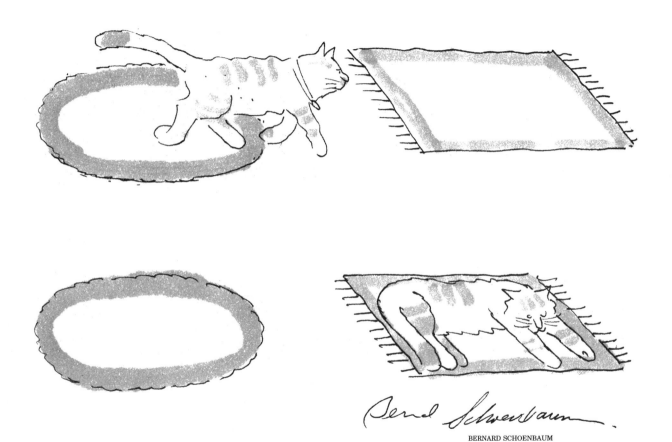

BERNARD SCHOENBAUM

VAHAN SHIRVANIAN

68

HENRY MARTIN

"I wrote a letter to the president of the company about the red food dye in your Turkey and Chicken Parts and he wrote back a two-page letter, the bottom line of which was something about consumerism, test marketing, and finicky eaters."

"You wouldn't be purring so smugly if you knew we were careening into poverty."

MORT GERBERG

69

"Look, I already have a cat clock, a cat calendar, cat cushions, and a cat lamp—so beat it."

MICHAEL MASLIN

THE PUSSYCAT OLYMPICS

71

S.GROSS

SAM GROSS

"According to the note, they voted 8 to 3
to come live with their father."

"What is it with you, anyway?"

FRANK MODELL
© 1985 The New Yorker Magazine, Inc.

"Sit up!"

"Lie down!"

"Heel!"

"Give a paw!"

"Roll over!"

"Congratulations, Mr. Stevens. Sally graduates *summa cum laude* from the Canby Cat Obedience School."

"I know it's not Perrier, but that's all that's available."

"Darn! We forgot the non-temperamental cats!"

"Cat out?"

MICHAEL CRAWFORD

GAHAN WILSON

"Here, puss, puss, puss!"

FELIPE GALINDO (FEGGO)

ARNIE LEVIN
© 1975 The New Yorker Magazine, Inc.

79

"I haven't been happy, but I pretend for her sake."

ED FRASCINO

VAHAN SHIRVANIAN

"Two martinis, very dry, one with an olive, one with a goldfish."

T. HAGGERTY   TIM HAGGERTY

JETÉ

BERNARD SCHOENBAUM

83

"City mouse, country mouse—
I'm not particular."

CHARLES SAUERS

"First the good news—kitty finally came home. . . ."

ORLANDO BUSINO

84

"Bank robbery, safe cracking, counterfeiting,
forgery, no, no, no . . . you had to become
a cat burglar!"

THOMAS CHENEY

STUART LEEDS

"Pegler drank a toast to Mrs. Pegler, then he drank a toast to each of Mrs. Pegler's thirteen cats. That's too damn many cats!"

GEORGE BOOTH

THE FOUR CAT BREEDS

Domestic Pettables

These cats can take as much affection
as you're willing to dish out. This
includes hugging by 2-year-olds.
They can be found anywhere and
everywhere. Look for the tell-tale
"I aim to please" expression and
congenital bow.

Complete Paranoids

These felines are rarely seen
except under furniture and in the
back of closets. You might have
one and not even know it.

Foreign Costabundles

$6,000.⁰⁰

True Costabundles are recognized by their subliminal pricetags and nitwit owners. They tend to do a lot of sleeping

Stranges

This unfortunate group appears mainly in cat shows and in the imaginations of people who think of themselves as "cat fanciers." Hairlessness, wrinkly skin, rat-tails, and weird facial expressions are a few of their attributes.

ROZ CHAST

JOHN CASSADY

"Just because he's been declawed—
don't think he's any less dangerous."

AARON BACALL

"She can't understand it. You're not shedding and she is."

ORLIN

RICHARD ORLIN

BILL WOODMAN

"I'll tell you one thing, Percy, there aren't many cats like you."

Edgar, please run down to the shopping center right away, and get some milk and cat food. Don't get canned tuna, or chicken, or liver, or any of those awful combinations. Shop around and get a surprise. The pussies like surprises."

BOOTH

93

HOURS OF FUN

MICK STEVENS

94

"You're getting fat, Jason, too fat to do anything."

BORIS DRUCKER

"Of course she's beautiful. She sleeps eighteen hours a day."

BERNARD SCHOENBAUM

97

"That's nothing. You should have been here five minutes ago when the dish ran away with the spoon."

HENRY MARTIN

98

"I tell you, the book has every-
thing—sex, history, conscious-
ness, and cats!"

WILLIAM HAMILTON

© 1977 The New Yorker Magazine, Inc.

COMPLAINTS

S. GROSS

SAM GROSS

1

2

3

4

5

6

VAHAN SHIRVANIAN

100

"Well, I hope you're proud of yourself!"

"We have fourteen cats, but Kevin thinks we only have twelve."

"Boots is getting too fat
to sleep on the car!"

DON OREHEK

"There, it's down! Now give her nine of these pills daily."

ORLANDO BUSINO

DEPOSIT BOX NOS. 150—200

STAMPS →

CALLAHAN

JOHN CALLAHAN

"Cats are *so* independent!"

"Pounce!"

CHARLES SAUERS

"Your cat is entering my sphere of influence!"

BORIS DRUCKER
© 1970 The New Yorker Magazine, Inc.

THE
Evolution
of
Catfish

JOHN S.P. WALKER

"I think he realizes what a lucky kitty he is."

LEE LORE

"I used to have lots of little pussycats, but I decided it was easier
to have one great big pussycat."

113

AARON BACALL

"That's a sacrilege!"

ANDY WYATT

"He really needs a bath but the tab on his collar says to dry clean only."

"We found her hiding
in one of the closets."

115

BERNARD SCHOENBAUM

JERRY MARCUS *Jerry Marcus*

"It seems the only thing you remembered to do around here was to put the cat out!"

"Yes, my darling—I *know* that Chessy is crying out for you—and so am *I!*"

MORT GERBERG

118

"You're going to have a nice long life and have lots of kittens. Now scat!"

BORIS DRUCKER

ARNOLDO FRANCHIONI

"They're Siamese cats."

J.J. SEMPÉ

"I didn't mind it so much before Flossy had kittens."

JOHN JONIK

MICHAEL MASLIN

Something the Cat Dragged In

"It's not that I don't trust you, Estelle, but before I eat this oatmeal
I want to see the box that it came in."

BUD GRACE